Word Families
Table Of Contents

"ab"

cab

crab

nab

lab

grab

"ad"

bad

glad

dad

pad

had

mad

"ag"

b**ag**

br**ag**

n**ag**

t**ag**

w**ag**

r**ag**

"am"

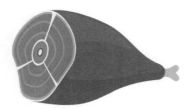

ham

jam

slam

yam

am

"an"

c an

p an

f an

r an

m an

t an

th an

"ap"

c ap

g ap

l ap

m ap

n ap

t ap

"at"

bat

sat

cat

hat

mat

pat

that

"ed"

fed

wed

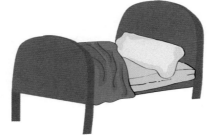

bed

led

red

"en"

hen

men

ten

pen

when

then

den

"et"

set

jet

pet

yet

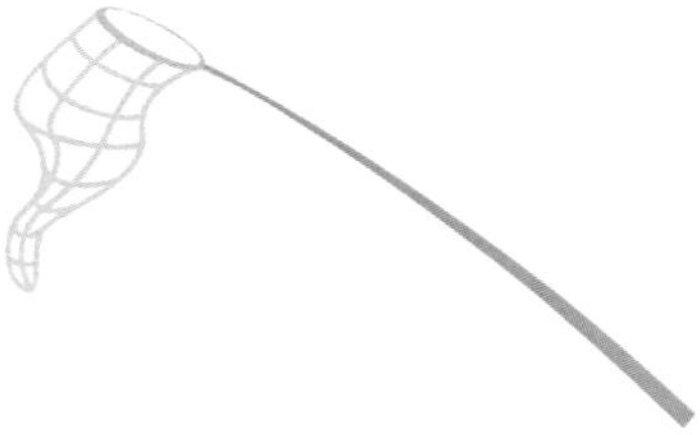

net

met

let

get

"ig"

big

dig

jig

pig

wig

"in"

bin

win

grin

twin

chin

pin

fin

"ip"

sip

dip

trip

hip

flip

rip

"it"

bit

split

hit

fit

pit

quit

sit

"ob"

job

slob

rob

blob

sob

mob

"og"

dog

frog

hog

log

jog

fog

"op"

cop

hop

drop

STOP

stop

shop

top

mop

"ot"

dot

got

pot

not

tot

hot

rot

"ub"

cub

hub

rub

tub

scrub

"ug"

bug

hug

dug

mug

jug

rug

tug

"un"

nun

fun

bun

sun

run

"ut"

hut

cut

gut

shut

nut

but

Made in the USA
Las Vegas, NV
18 October 2023